River Of Living Light

Jump Into the River
Go With the Flow

NadjaMedia.com

Nadja Media
530 Los Angeles Ave., Suite 115
Moorpark, California 93021

ISBN-10: 1-942057-06-7
ISBN-13: 978-1-942057-06-2

Cover art by Judy Bullard www.jaebeecreations.com

Copyright © 2011 by Nadja.

All rights reserved. No part of this book may be reproduced by any mechanical, photographic, or electronic process, or in the form of a phonographic recording; nor may it be stored in a retrieval system, transmitted, or otherwise be copied for public or private use—other than for "fair use" as brief quotations embodied in articles and reviews—without prior written permission of the publisher.

This is a work of fiction. Names, characters, places, and incidents either are a product of the author's imagination or are used fictitiously, and any resemblance to actual persons, living or dead, business establishments, events, or locales is entirely coincidental. No liability is assumed for damages resulting from the use of or misinterpretation of information contained herein. Nadja never advocates the use of violence in any form.

The author of this book is not a doctor and does not dispense medical advice or prescribe the use of any technique as a form of treatment for physical, emotional, or medical problems without the advice of a physician, either directly or indirectly. The intent of the author is only to offer information of a general nature to help you in your quest for emotional and spiritual well-being. In the event you use any of the information in this book for yourself, the author and publisher assume no responsibility for your actions. If expert assistance or counseling is needed, the services of a competent professional should be sought.

Reader Comments on River Of Living Light

An invitation to meet your soul. *Sandy J.*

It made me want to stand up and shout, "Hallelujah!" *Jakki H.*

The excitement and energy kept me reading as it infused me with waves of Light. An activation and pathway (portal) to allow more Light into our lives. *Anita L.*

I can see this in self - help groups. *SamKaia*

A love letter to humanity. I wish I could have read this during my teenage years. It reminds me of the Desiderata – timeless. *Marilyn F.*

Everything I believe put into one small package. Just one verse a day would keep me going in a positive direction. *Anna C.*

Potent. I would love to see people who have lost their way or those who envision doom and gloom for the future read this little gem and practice what it suggests. *Omanasa*

Dedication

This book is dedicated to the Great Spirit, Mother Earth, Brother Sun, Grandmother Moon, and Father Sky in gratitude for their sustenance. They are the Supreme Givers without which we would not know Life.

— Nadja

Acknowledgments

With gratitude to Mt. Shasta

and the Natural World.

Introduction

You are born with all you need to live a life of fulfillment. Are you seeking outside yourself for answers, hope, peace, love? This book shows you how to connect up with your real self who can guide you to become the authentic person you were meant to be. Yes, you can be in the driver's seat on the path to unlock your greatest gifts and ride the waves into the future with self-confidence.

This missal was written to share hope, direction, and vision with people all over the Earth during this challenging but exciting Time of Change. May the words of this book enter your spirit, renew your mind, open your heart, enlighten your soul, and give you Life. Hear the sound of the river and feel its energy as you read or listen.

Inspiration

"There is a river flowing now very fast. It is so great and swift that there are those who will be afraid. They will try to hold on to the shore. They will feel they are being torn apart and will suffer greatly. Know the river has its destination. The elders say we must let go of the shore, push off into the middle of the river, keep our eyes open, and our heads above the water."

— Anonymous

"We are the ones
we have been waiting for."

— Author Unknown

Caution All Readers

The River of Light is not a real river with water. It is a spirit river. Do not jump into a real river and end your life. You need to graduate from Earth School with your Certificate of Completion at your God-ordained not self-determined time. The author accepts no liability for those who misinterpret these words and tragically end their lives because of the content of this book.

River Of Living

Light

Jump Into the River

Go With the Flow

We are the ones

Who have passed on before

And are counting on you

To open the Door

To open the Door

To the New Time to Come

When humankind can flourish

And bury the gun

Go With the Flow

A glorious future awaits you

Wake up, join forces

With those who surround you

Don't count any losses

Awake Brothers and Sisters

Jump into the flow

Let go of the past

And all that you know

A New Time is coming

Nothing is lost

Jump into the River

Don't think of the cost

This act will pay dividends

Beyond our wildest dreams

Hope is alive

Life's not what it seems

The matrix is ending

It's collapsing so fast

Jump into the River

Let go of the past

The past doesn't serve you

Let the dead bury the dead

Your future's before you

Look ahead, look ahead

The Earth will restore

Humanity will thrive

You'll be fully awake

And totally alive

Don't be discouraged

Don't take your life

Glory awaits you

The end of all strife

Death is a great teacher

It is a true friend

But not to be experienced

Till your assigned end

No harm to others

No harm to self

Stay on the Path

Find the True Wealth

You're powerful, miraculous

Beyond what you know

But blind to your potential

And the seeds you can sow

Stay on your case

Do your deep Inner Work

It's difficult but worth it

Responsibilities don't shirk

Overcome your addictions

Drugs, alcohol, and the rest

They numb you to your hurt

And cover up your distress

Acknowledge your anger,

Your sadness, your pain

Hear them out fully

Let your Inner Being reign

Have the courage

To face it full on

Stay with the course

From dusk until dawn

The energy you have

Once you clean up your mess

Will amaze and impress you

You'll live without stress

The goal of this Work

Is that once you are done

You no longer react

The Battle is won

A Soul well cleansed

From the dirt and the grime

Becomes a sparkling, clear diamond

Like coal does in time

Recognize your faults

Sweep your own doorstep clean

Clear the cobwebs from your mind

Let your True Self be seen

During the course of our life

We meet those we don't like

They're our best teachers of love

Providing Insight

Judging is puzzling

And tricky, too

What you see outside

Mirrors you

Ask Truth to reveal

What you see and hear

No false assumptions

No fantasy or fear

See clear without filters

That distort what you see

So you can see perfectly

What is and be free

When caught up with problems

Face to face

View them as lessons

In compassion and grace

GO WITH THE FLOW

Sometimes you're so busy

Inside your own head

You miss everything

Around you instead

The mind is always active

It can steal your life

By continually repeating

And creating more strife

Jump into the River

Let go of the past

It will carry you forward

This pain will not last

Accept the whole self

Shadow and all

Embrace all that you've done

Love self and stand tall

Review your whole life

All relationships you've had

In Truth see your part

Both the good and the bad

It doesn't really matter

Where you've been

The most important trip

Is deep down within

Your True Self forgives you

For whatever you've done

It understands why

And celebrates lessons won

Clean up your own act

Do your own Work first

With your small self reformed

You help the New World birth

Go With the Flow

It's easier to be angry

Than to face fear or pain

Surrender, do the Work

Authenticity you'll gain

Authentic means genuine

To Thine own self be true

Standing solid as a rock

Being the real you

Work through your anger

Release sadness and pain

Forgiveness is key

No judgment or blame

Dance it out, Shake it out

Drum it out, Shout

When the false self leaves

You will KNOW and not doubt

Worry is a killer

Just like a knife

It cuts you off from the Present

And causes strife

You are not what you think

Don't believe your mind

It's the Supreme Trickster

And will keep you blind

Learn to watch yourself thinking

See the ticker tape pass

Until you notice yourself noticing

Getting caught in the trap

Grow where you're planted

Take in the Light

Nourish yourself wholly

Welcome Insight

You are worthy, you are worthy

You are worthy beyond measure

Your Inner Being is

An absolute treasure

The Pearl of Great Price

Lies deep in your heart

Dig way down within

To realize your part

Don't give away your power

To let another decide

Which way you should go

And then choose to abide

You are responsible

For the life that you live

However you live it

Your consent you give

Be the Captain of your Ship

The Guardian of your Soul

With the pure Light inside you

Love yourself Whole

Take your own counsel

Let your Inner Voice speak

It has all the answers

To the questions you seek

Who knows you better

Than your own Self and Soul

Who's lived with you intimately

As the years come and go?

All you need to know

Was given at birth

Just uncover and discover

Your true Inner Worth*

No money to exchange

No books to read

No teachers to tell you

What you need

You are the Watcher

You are the Guru

You are your best teacher

Gee, you are you (G-U-R-U)

Awake Brothers and Sisters

Use your mind as a tool

Do your Inner Work to tame it

Let your heart and soul rule

You've been programmed by your country

The media, your mind

Your parents, your schooling

And most humankind

Step out of your old self

Step into the new

Erase all your patterns

Be the Real You

The world that surrounds you

Is not what it seems

It is changing so fast

It is like a bad dream

Stay calm through upheavals

Of society and Mother Earth

So you will survive

To witness total rebirth

When the Darkness comes

Gather family and kin

Rejoice and be happy

New Earth will begin

A New Day is dawning

Duality will end

Peace will blanket the Planet

We will ascend

A New World awaits you

Celebrate and live

Take the High Road and know

That the angels will give

Go With the Flow

You the stamina to live

Through these tumultuous times

When polarity dies

And the Shift supplies

All the upgrades you need

In order to succeed

As a species renewed

Chains dropped, consciousness pursued

Planet Earth is a jewel

In this Great Universe

It is Coming of Age

Destruction will reverse

At long last we've made it

Through the muck and the slime

To a New Earth unfolding

That's outside of time

Duality will become

A thing of the past

The Dark had its way

But no longer can last

Don't believe what you see

Or trust what you hear

It's delusion and illusion

The End Time's so near

A New Day is dawning

Look deeply within

Merge with the Self

Release what you've been

Celebrate the time

When the craziness will end

Dance in the knowingness

That Spirit will descend

The Light will take over

The Dark will be gone

Humanity will flourish

You will Sing your True Song

Have faith that the plan

Unfolding before you

Is perfectly timed

And planned to restore you

Tame your mind

And you will find

With Heaven on Earth

You then align

The Planet is changing

Transmuting and evolving

Galactic transmissions

Our problems are solving

Look up and live

In gratitude and praise

Use these emotions

Your frequency to raise

Your smile is beautiful

Your smile is bright

Smile often from the heart

It's a Beacon of Light

Step out of your blindness

See with your third eye

It will reveal the truth

And will never lie

The truth of the matter

Is that you are One

With everything else

Including the Sun

Go With the Flow

Go out into Nature

Replenish and renew

Listen to the Sound

It'll totally heal you

Learn to love yourself truly

Love others too

Include all the Beings

That are around you

If we all do these things

We can pass through the Change

With joy and thanksgiving

And the least amount of pain

Start envisioning the world

You want to live in

Attitude is everything

Outside and within

Heaven on Earth

Will happen, you'll see

This change is imminent

Just learn how to Be

Forgive self and others

No judgment, no blame

Liberation's so near

It knows you by name

The Power within

Is being revved up each day

Just open your heart

And get out of the way

Get out of the way

So you can receive

Sacred Starseed Transmissions

That you will need

To fly free as the Eagle

With the all-seeing eye

Feet on the ground

Your spirit soaring high

Mother Nature will teach you

What you need to know

Praise her, protect her

Restore her and grow

Your time to blossom

Has come at long last

Jump into the River

Let go of the past

It'll sweep you along

To a land never seen

Communicate with Nature

Just like in a dream

Go With the Flow

When you entertain fear

No Truth will you find

Fear paralyzes the body

And terrorizes the mind

You are in charge

Of what you think

Let dark thoughts pass through

Then you won't sink

Go With the Flow

Let go of the fear

That keeps you stuck

It twists your perception

And runs you amuck

Your body is your temple

Your own sacred space

Appreciate and thank it

For it's truth, love, and grace

Go With the Flow

Honor your father

Honor your mother

They gave you your body

That's like none other

Without this equipment

You couldn't grow

On Planet Earth

To learn and to Know

Eat foods from Nature

Get sunshine each day

Exercise, breathe deeply,

Keep dis-ease away

It's time to come out

Not play a role

Be who you are

True to your soul

Learn to be comfortable

Within your own skin

Release all concern

About fat and thin

Take off the mask

Get out of the parade

Be the real you

Don't be afraid

Go With the Flow

It's not about drugs

It's not about pot

It's about doing the Deep Work

To stop being what you're not

Drop your chains

Break out of your shell

Step out into freedom

From your self-made hell

Walk fully upright

With freedom and grace

An integrated Human Being

A new species, a new race

Inside your own skin

You are a free being

Don't be afraid

To be truly seen

Life's an inside job

Be tough and be tender

Search your mind and your heart

Then totally surrender

Say no to distractions

Be firm, claim your space

Seek quietude daily

Slow down your fast pace

You were born with talent

Usually more than just one

Find out what they are

Create and have fun

Discover your passion

Follow your bliss

Become who you are

What joy is this

Play and be happy

That's what's required

To help self and others

Become rewired

What's the point

To sacrifice the soul

Just for money in the bank

And to pay the toll?

Go With the Flow

Don't be what you have

You are not what you own

You are who you are

Without bank, job, or home

You must attend

The University within

This is the Knowledge

You can't get in college**

Don't count on others

Count yourself in

Be your own best friend

Through the thick and the thin

Look into the mirror

Greet who you see

Look deep into your eyes

And love yourself free

Turn on the Switch

Turn on the Light

Your House will be clear

Your House will be bright

Whoever's before you

Give them freedom to be

Accept them, love them

They will heal naturally

Go With the Flow

If you want to have friends

Learn to be a friend

It all depends on you

And the vibes you send

Have integrity

Stick to your word

Then when you speak

You'll be fully heard

Go With the Flow

Be alert to your thoughts

The words that you say

They are the essence

That creates your day

Respect others' bodies

Respect your own

It's none other than

Your palace, your home

The healing power of touch

Human skin to skin

Gives opportunity to communicate

From without to within

This need not be sexual

With silent, pure love

The magic of touch

Transmits healing from Above

Go With the Flow

Take your inner child with you

Wherever you go

Love and protect her

Good seeds you will sow

These seeds will bear fruit

Wherever you are

Their effect on others

Will spread wide and far

Count your blessings

Every day

Stay in gratitude

This is the Way

Each moment you live

Become deeply engaged

Say goodbye to the fear,

The sadness, and rage

Say hello to the laughter,

The joy, and the Light

The Gift of today

Is such a delight

This is the Work

You can do for Planet Earth

To help It along

And hasten rebirth

Walk with confidence

Hold your head high

You are a Star Being

That came from the sky

Find the Thread

Follow it back through Time

Erase every particle

The Freedom is Divine

Step into the Energy

That Creates and Flows

Become One with It

Your Spirit knows

You were born

For a Time such as this

To develop your strength

And expand your bliss

Awake Brothers and Sisters

Jump into the flow

Let go of the past

And of all that you know

Just the Beginning and not the End

Be still and know that

I am God (within you).

Psalm 46:10

Neither shall they say, Lo here! or, lo there! for,

behold, the Kingdom of God

is within you.

Luke 17:21

Afterword

Row, row, row your boat

Gently down the stream

Merrily, merrily, merrily, merrily

Life is but a dream

Endnote 1

*After you have worked on yourself according to the guidance given in this book, you could take one, two, three or more consecutive days off. You will know when the time is right. (Before you begin, thoroughly discuss this with your doctor and follow his or her advice. Do not discontinue prescription drugs unless you have your doctor's permission to do so. The writer accepts no liability for not consulting your doctor before you begin or for not following the doctor's orders.) Prepare your food ahead of time----3 simple meals of natural ingredients daily with adequate water. Just sit alone with yourself in silence----no TV, computer, phone, or any other distractions. Use earplugs if necessary. Sit still in silence and DO NOTHING (no meditation, writing, reading, art, etc.). Just breathe naturally. Let everything go and forget everything you learned. Get acquainted with the real you. The results are deeply satisfying, liberating yet calming, and border on the miraculous. If you do not get these results then go back to the instructions in this book and do more emotional clearing and then try again. Emotional cleansing takes time, patience, hard work, alertness, and strength. For some this process could take years. Feel your feelings until they feel themselves totally out of your body. Stay with it because you are releasing at the cellular level. It could take hours. Don't allow distractions during this process. It is not necessary to analyze the feelings or their origins. This is not mind work but soul work to clear the mind and body. When triggered emotionally, consider it a gift. Try to process the feelings immediately. We are NOT our feelings. Everyday stand in front of a mirror and say the words, "I am a free Soul."

Endnote 2

**Please note that I am not against schooling and higher education. On the contrary, I believe these can be extremely valuable experiences as long as the students and teachers take this process seriously. Education can expand the horizon and stimulate the mind. It can also create a wonderful foundation upon which to build a successful life. However, our current education system (with a few exceptions) does not encourage the student to discover the Knowledge within, become Self-Realized, or to wake the Soul to Its full height. Education of the future will be holistic and will produce loving, well-balanced, emotionally sound, physically healthy, fully conscious human beings who can operate at their full potential. There will be no more separation of mind, body, nature, and spirit.

Inspiration and Door-Openers

The Bible, Jesus the Christ, Abraham, Moses, Mt. Shasta, Upper Panther Meadow, Braco, Prem Rawat, Lake Siskiyou, Yogananda's Encinitas Garden, Harbin Hot Springs, Founders Grove, Big Sur, Pt. Lobos State Park, Cambria, The Grand Tetons, Estes Park, Silverton, Bryce Canyon, Ludington, Sangamon River, Chumash Interpretive Center, Satwiwa, Wildwood, Connecticut in October, Long Island in Spring, Kabir, Radha Soami Satsang Beas, Sufi Dancing, Erik Satie, SARK, Beethoven, Mozart, Bach, Moldau (Smetana),

Brahms, Chopin, Sergei Rachmaninoff, Franz Schubert, Pyotr Ilyich Tchaikovsky, Anton Chekov, Padre Pio, St. Andrew's Abbey, Debussy, Questhaven Retreat, Isak Dinesen, Sulamith Wolfing, Muktananda, The Rebbe, Kahlil Gibran, Rembrandt, Sister Corita Kent, Dr. Seuss, Abbott and Costello, Mr. Bean, Peter Sellers, Charlie Chaplin, Isadora Duncan, Emily Dickinson, Marie Curie, Joan of Ark, Sacajawea, Hildegard de Bingen, Mother Theresa, Saint Therese Little Flower, Amma, Esther, Dhyani Ywahoo, Kathie Kolwitz, Anne Frank, Ann Wigmore, Prison Ashram Project, *David and Lisa*, Edith Piaf, *La Strada*, Marcel Marceau, *The Red Balloon*, <u>La Petit Prince</u>, fluorite, Moldavite, Labradorite, Lemurian Crystals, conch, Ruth Stout, cob houses, Luther Burbank, yurts, sun ovens, portals, vortexes, iPhones, Apple Computers, Optimum Health Institute, Avila Hot Springs, Inn of the Seventh Ray, Rassouli, Dandelion root powder, Nettle, Hawthorne, Red Root, Oat Straw, Purslane, Dudlia, Prickly Pear, HerbPharm, Elkhorn Slough, praying mantises, George Washington Carver, Simon Bolivar, the Elder Brothers, Lake Titicaca, Machu Pichu, Munay-Ki, ocarinas, drums, wind harp, dulcimer, didgeridoo, alpine flowers, California poppy and purple lupine, Mule Ears, Lily of the Valley, lilac, columbine, Ojo Caliente, Trinity Alps, Lewiston, Weaverville, Arcata, Ashland, Compassion, ecstatic dancing, Qi Gong, City of 10,000

Buddhas, Victoria (Canada), Greece, REI, Vibram FiveFingers, Cannon Digital Elf, Jalama Beach, papaya digestive enzymes, acorn mush, maiden hair fern, quaking aspen, weeping willow, oaks, birch, dogwood, redbud, maple, killdeer, wood duck, humming bird, cardinal, house wren, Joan Baez, Bob Dylan, Babaji, organic gardening, Yeats, permaculture, Paul Stamets, Aldo Leopold, Meditation Mount, Krotona Library, Halcyon, Dr. Bernard Jensen, Dr. Bronner, Robert Frost, *Swan Lake*, *My Fair Lady*, *Wizard of Oz*, *Singing in the Rain*, *The Sound of Music*, *ET*, Farmer and the Cook, Krishnamurti, Teilhard de Chardin, Ravi Shankar, Segovia, HeartMath, orbs, slant board, Vilcabamba, Marx Brothers, Nicholas Tesla,

Lime Kiln, *Hallelujah Chorus*, Four Corners, Patrick's Point, John Muir, Rabindranath Tagore, Hafiz, Immanuel Velikovsky, Buckminster Fuller, raw cacao beans, Esther Williams, Eckhart Tolle, Dr. John Christopher, Chief Seattle, Black Elk, Christa McAuliffe, Dr. Charles Saunders (D.C.), Patch Adams, Maria Treben, Jim Trelease, Carla Emery, Roger Tory Peterson, Master Lam Kam Chuen, Norman Walker, Michael Sandler, David Tralle, Outward Bound, Debbie Ford, Summerhill, Jeff Primack, Gurmukh, Axolotls, Confucius, Maurice Maeterlinck, youth hostels, Drunvalo Melchizedek, Leonardo Da Vinci, Michelangelo, Price Pottenger Foundation, United Plant Savers, Susun Weed, Hilarion, The

Insect World of J. Henri Fabre, We're All Doing Time, Be Here Now, Chop Wood Carry Water, The Power of Positive Thinking, Autobiography of a Yogi, Family Under the Bridge, Daniel Boone, Jack LaLane, Thich Nhat Hanh, Langston Hughes, Wanda Landowski, Bertrand Russell, Lao-Tse, Eric Hoffer, Rebazar Tarzs, Erma Bombeck, Art Buchwald, Edgar Cayce, Shri Yukteswar, Shams of Tabriz, Ibsen, Margaret Meade, Badger Claws, Manly P. Hall, Oprah, Art Bell, George Noory, Sylvia Ashton Warner, Natalie Goldberg, color indigo, newts, Art Linkletter, Red Skelton, Lucille Ball, Houdini, Ramana Maharshi, Chunyi Lin, Salvation Army, Florence Nightingale, Kathryn Kuhlman, Rod Serling, Marshall Field

Department Store, Einstein, *Scientific American*, *Omni*, *National Geographic*, *Mother Earth News*, Wisdom of the Earth Aromatherapy, <u>Elements of Style</u>, *Popular Mechanics*, *Harpers*, *Atlantic Monthly*, Henry David Thoreau, Ralph Waldo Emerson, Joel Goldsmith, Rudyard Kipling, Robert Louis Stevenson, William Wordsworth, Maria Alice Campos Freire, Findhorn, Rainer Maria Rilke, Hanna Kroeger, F. M. Houston (D.C.), Max Gerson (M.D.), Emmet Fox, Ernest Holmes, St. Benedict, Christopher Nyerges, <u>Slim Spurling's Universe</u>, J. I. Rodale, Dannion Brinkley, Olga Worrall, Herbert Spencer Zim, Adali Stevenson, Vita Mix, Nutri Bullet, Dr. Laura Schlessinger, Allen Alexander Milne, <u>Man's Search for Meaning</u>,

Beatrix Potter, The Wind in the Willows, King Solomon's Ring, Amnesty International, wild foods, dark leafy greens, American Land Trust, Paracelsus, Galen, Hippocrates, Martin Luther King, Louis Pasteur, Galileo, Mutant Messenger Down Under, Honda Element, Nature Conservancy, Regenerative Design Institute, Patricia Cota-Robles, Louise Hay, A Course in Miracles, Cory Herter, The International Council of Thirteen Indigenous Grandmothers, Joseph Campbell, Jean Houston, Rudolf Steiner, Alexis Carrel, The Artist's Way, The Dancing Healers, Dr. Nick Begich, Jr., The Hiding Place by Corrie Ten Boom, From Concentration Camp to Concert Hall by Shony Alex Braun, Bartholomew Cubbins, Chaplain Ray

Hoekstra's books, Coast to Coast Radio Program, Peace Corps, CCC, Atlantis, Lemuria, Planet Yachats, Pleiades, Le Creuset, Staub, Fontignac, Lodge, IDOS, All-Clad, Pyrex, Snowpeak, Greyhound Bus, Martin Luther King, Jr., Chief Joseph, Ishi, Peter Max, wind chimes, Christmas Cactus, bamboo clothing, Patagonia base layers, Smartwool, turquoise, Tribest, fenugreek sprouts, Olympic Peninsula, honey bees, David Wolfe, Pt. Dume, ethnobotany, Audubon Society, community gardens, food co-ops, Energy Essentials, Earth Shift Products, Botija black olives, chaga, reishi mushroom, noni, pomegranate, chia seeds, goji berries, cayenne pepper, seaweed, almonds, sunflower seeds, hemp, astragalus, lentils, turmeric, mangosteen, wheatgrass, cinnamon, ginger, peppermint, onion, celery, apple, dates, pecans, wild caught salmon, beets, organic corn, broccoli, squash, garlic, oats, millet, spelt, quinoa, caraway seeds, celery seeds, yams, basil, fennel, cumin, black cod, walnuts, teff, injera, sesame seeds, pumpkin seeds, eyes, Kinship with All Life, Crazy Horse, YMCA, Boy Scouts, Girl Scouts, ice, malva, raw pickles, fiver.com, sesame oil, horseradish, raw honey, raw apple cider vinegar, sun baths, Ringing Cedars book series, homemade sauerkraut, yogurt, dal, clover sprouts, mung bean sprouts, The Maker's Diet by Jordan Rubin, Rumi, John Graham Lake, Joni Eareckson Tada, Rabbit Stick, Cry Beloved Country, Shakespeare, Iliad and

Odyssey, international folk dancing, clogging, belly dancing, chameleons, painted turtles, wood cock, Farley Mowat, J.A. Henckels knives, sardines, Mark Twain, Royal Raymond Rife, Berbere spice mix, guitar, Nick Vujicic, <u>Bhagavad Gita</u>, mycology, <u>The Hobbit</u>, whales, dolphins, People's Organic Food Cooperative, egret, buckwheat lettuce, Deer Park, sea otters, bluebirds, shiitake mushrooms, The Farm in Tennessee, <u>Nourishing Traditions</u> by Sally Fallon, seed cheese, congee, <u>Stalking the Wild Asparagus</u> by Euell Gibbons, elephant seals, adzuki beans, rainbows, waterfalls, brooks, rivers, Pascalite Clay, gynostemma, ume plum, blue-green algae, moss, Jill Bolte Taylor, selinite, oil of oregano, Inelia Benz, Mashhur Anam,

Christel Hughes, Terri and Robert Talltree, Ronda del Boccio, Master Chungliang Al Huang, Raw Food World, Cultures for Health, NuWave ovens, Perfect Pickler, Body Ecology, Savory Lotus, Dawn Clark, Debra Cummings, GoPro Camera, Dr. Emoto, homemade chicken bone and beef bone gelatin, Fissler Pressure Cookers, Dr. Zhi Gang Sha, Dr. Bhagat Singh Thind, beet kvass, preserved lemons, Jim Self, Dolores Cannon, Luis Fernando Mostajo Maertens, Sunray Kelly, Dr. Sarah Larsen, BioLumina Spirulina, NextworldTV.com, kikisays.com, YouTube, lamb quarters, turmeric root, raw pressed cane juice, quinoa rejuvelac, Herkimer Diamonds, Arkansas quartz crystals, Cell Salts, Celtic Salt, neem, oyster mushrooms, miso, sourdough, iPod, castor oil, clove, kitchari, The Apple Store, Bookaholic, VitaClay Smart Organic Multicooker, Carol Tuttle, Neale Donald Walsch, Enya, Yma Sumac, Donna Eden, Elle Febbo, Bradley Nelson, John Newton, Lynn Waldrop, Mas Sajady, NPR, The Great Books, Ken Stone, Garage Band, Apple Care, fresh curry leaves, Anais Ninn, Rachael Carson, Grandma Moses, Jill Jackson, Mike Dooley, Barry Long, Marjory Wildcraft, Spring Forest Qi Gong, Chief Golden Light Eagle, Christine Day, All American Sun Oven, Scott Werner, M.D., Patty Greer, iands.org, TED Talks, Goldfish Reports, Magenta Pixie, GeoEngineeringWatch.com, David Wilcock,

Jean Houston, Raw Food World, Vilcabamba, Kogi People, Bhutan.

Parting Words from the Author

For years I was searching

And developing my mind

But unfortunately I left

My heart behind

It was frozen in ice

Since I was a kid

I was a loner

And retreated and hid

My beauty of youth

Was never shared

My Soul in friendship

Never bared

Parting Words from the Author

I imprisoned myself

And threw away the key

Usurping my Earth life

Being heartless with me

This situation seemed easier

Than entanglements of heart

But in truth what it did

It tore me apart

Feeling empty and lost

No core anymore

I started from scratch

To connect and restore

Parting Words from the Author

To process my feelings

More years it took

To realize my worth

As explained in this book

Then one day I met

A friend I could trust

She saw my True Heart

Behind all the rust

She was patient and wise

And stuck by my side

While I worked hard on my issues

My pain and my pride

Parting Words from the Author

She applauded my progress

As I journeyed along

Till the day I emerged

To sing my True Song

Without a good friend

We can never become

A real human being

Able to love and have fun

I've put my life back together

I now have the key

My mind, heart, and Soul

Work in close harmony

Parting Words from the Author

This book was written

For you and me

To reclaim our lives

And our humanity

Resources

Helpguide.org—Free resources to help you resolve mental and emotional health issues. Includes hotlines and support groups. Helps you help yourself and others.

FoodBabe.com

Mercola.com

NaturalNews.com

Bioneers.org

WestonPrice.org

NextWorldTV.com

MagentaPixie.com

ScottWerner.org

RingingCedars.com

PattyGreer.com

iands.org

Findhorn.org

Cohousing.org

Nature.org

Crimes Against Nature
by Robert F. Kennedy

Cosmic Ordering Made Easier
by Ellen Watts

M. T. Keshe

Santos Bonacci

Dr. Masaru Emoto

Vandana Shiva

Jean Houston

Masanobu Fukuoka

Chunyi Lin

Susun Weed

Tusli Gabbard

Paul Stamets

Buckmaster Fuller

David Wilcock

Matt Kahn

Chief Golden Light Eagle

Christine Day

Lynn Waldrop

John Newton

Christel Hughes

Debora Wayne

Tarek Bibi

Lanna Spencer

Sophia Zoe

Jo Dunning

Lisa Transcendence Brown

Julie Renee

Eckhart Tolle

Neale Donald Walsch

Stacey Mayo

Dorian Light

Lottie Cooper

Andie DePass

Judy Cali

Marianne Williamson

Dr. Madlena Kantscheff

Dipal Shah

Peta Amber Lynne

Anamika

Sarah Lynn Kennedy

Emmanuel Dagher

Jenny Ngo

Anah Maa

Delores Cannon

Jarrad Hewett

Tamra Oviatt

Cathy Hohmeyer

Morry Zelcovitch

Rassouli

Akiane Kramarik

SARK

Shiloh Sophia

Aviva Gold

Ho'oponopono

The Emotion Code by Bradley Nelson

Emotional Freedom Technique (EFT)

Acim.org

Wopg.org

BirthingAndRebirthing.com

YouWealthRevolution.com

FromHeartacheToJoy.com

AcousticHealth.com

GalacticConnection.com

GeoEngineeringWatch.org

NotesFromTheUniverse.com

Homeopathic Cell Salts

TED Talks

OptimumHealthInstitute.com

NewPhoenixRising.com

About The Author

After working many years in the public sector Nadja is reinventing herself as an artist and writer. She has an eclectic background. Her joys include adventuring on the Open Road, dancing, cooking, being in nature, writing and painting. She is also interested in natural building, organic gardening, alternative health, life-long learning, travel, and living moment to moment. Nadja writes for the conscious community and people who are interested in healing, meditation, transformation, ascension, and the New Earth. This includes highly sensitive people, Starseeds, Indigos, empaths, Light Workers, energy healers, artists, visionaries, and those in recovery and discovery.

Also By Author

Soft-cover books, eBooks, MP3s, and CDs Smashwords, Amazon, Kindle, CreateSpace, CDBaby, iTunes, YouTube, and your local bookstore by request.

River of Living Light

Evolution Revolution

Random Thoughts and Poems

Hopi Blue Corn

El Maiz Azul de los Hopis

Visionary Tales for the New Earth

Color Me Bright Coloring Book

Blue Sky

Ascension Codes

Raps, Chants, and Rants

Women's Power Awakened

Ozzengoggle Poems

From the City of Shem

You Are Not Alone

Family Secrets

Flying Heart

Bullies

www.ingramcontent.com/pod-product-compliance
Lightning Source LLC
Chambersburg PA
CBHW070549050426
42450CB00011B/2789